CARROT TOP's
Junk in the Trunk

SOME ASSEMBLY REQUIRED

A FIRESIDE BOOK
PUBLISHED BY SIMON & SCHUSTER

FIRESIDE
Rockefeller Center
1230 Avenue of the Americas
New York, NY 10020

FIRESIDE and colophon are registered trademarks of Simon & Schuster Inc.

Designed by Robert Bull Design
Photographs by Deborah Triplett
Drawings by Steven R. Greenway

Manufactured in the United States of America

1   3   5   7   9   10   8   6   4   2

Library of Congress Cataloging-in-Publication Data
Thompson, Scott.
Carrot Top's junk in the trunk : some assembly required / by Scott Thompson.
p.   cm.
"A Fireside book."
1. Inventions.   I. Title.
T212. T47   1996

608—dc20   96-29047
                                                                           CIP.

ISBN 0-684-81429-3

ACKNOWLEDGMENTS

Thanks to Brad Greenberg, Ken Phillips, Mel Berger, Mike August, Jeff Robinov, Peter Nelson, Eric Godfrey, Deborah Triplett, Ron Hardman, Tom Haines, Jennifer Stieber, Steve Greenway, Dominick Anfuso, Cassie Jones . . .

And special thanks to Charles Viracola.

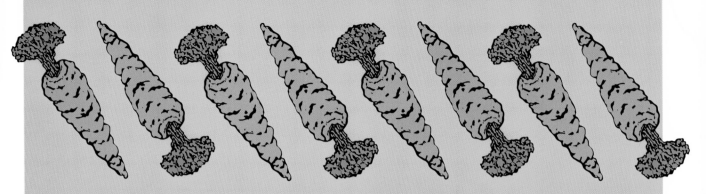

To my family,
my friends
. . . and all my fans!

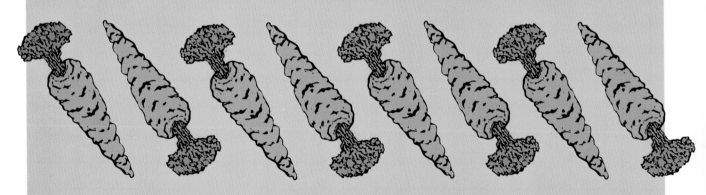

(You know who you are.)

JUNK IN THE trunk. A phrase my friends use affectionately in describing my act. But there is more to it than meets the eye. My inventions are the culmination of years of research in the fields of physics, chemistry, aerodynamics, anthropology, psychoanalysis, metallurgy, metrology! . . . okay, I didn't buy that one either, but it sounds good. You've heard the saying, "One man's junk is another man's jewel." Well, that doesn't just apply to my love life. It's my life story as well. Junk is junk unless you do something with it. That's why I put this book together, to show you how to transform your junk into fun, useful jewels, just like I do.

However, first I have to let you in on my secret. Promise not to tell? Okay, it's twist ties and duct tape. Shhhh! Don't say it too loud. Well, there you have it . . .

Illustrations by Steven Greenway

the Big Secret of the Top Family. The cat's out of the trunk, so to speak. Those are the two things that can transform junk into jewels and change lives forever. If you look closely at the pictures ahead, you can see that these two things, twist ties and duct tape, truly hold the fibers of my life together. When combined with a little imagination, they can brighten up your day as well.

I discovered this secret years ago, when I was but a wee carrot. You see, I didn't start out as the handsome comic movie idol you will see in the pages to come. I was once a real carrot. No, you didn't read it wrong, I did say real carrot. That's how I got my name (and you probably thought it was just the hair)—but I'll get back to that later.

First things first. I can't figure out why no one believes that

I grew up as a real carrot. I mean, it fits, doesn't it? What else could I have been—a cabbage, a rutabaga? Have you ever seen an orange rutabaga? That's what I thought. So you see, it's really not that odd.

I remember it like it was yesterday . . . (dreamy special effects music). Come on, use your imagination! Okay . . . ahhh, now that's better. I was born in a lovely vegetable patch in sunny Florida to two upstanding parents. They loved and cared for me very much.

My mother was the prettiest carrot in the whole patch, and smart, too. She would tell me all kinds of things, for example that human parents are wrong—eating carrots won't improve your eyesight. After all, she is a carrot, and it hadn't helped her eyesight one bit.

Illustrations by Steven Greenway

My father was the first carrot ever to work for NASA (keep that imagination going—you've come this far). His dream was to put a carrot on the moon. He often said that if the moon were really made of cheese, then a few carrots would make it a much better party tray. I know, I never understood that either. Maybe dyslexia wasn't his only problem!

My parents always stressed that a good education is very important, but school wasn't easy for me. Imagine being the only carrot on the school bus, not to mention the lunchroom.

I have one brother. He's brave and strong. Whenever I ran into trouble in the patch he would always save me. One time, he beat up three whole potatoes from one of the big city rows. Later, he joined the Air Force, making the whole patch proud.

Well, I guess that just leaves me and my story. I always wanted to be a performer. I was bitten by the show business bug at a young age. One summer, when I was working as a busboy at a dinner theater in New York, Orson Welles thought I was part of his dinner salad and took a bite. I barely escaped, but from that moment on I knew my calling.

I tried many different jobs in the entertainment industry. I was a rodeo clown for a while, until I realized that horses and carrots don't mix. I tried opera, but it made me nervous to be in a room with all those hungry overweight people. I even tried to be an Elvis impersonator in Las Vegas, but I was just too thin to fit into the sequined jumpsuit. I had all but given up on showbiz and got a job at a hardware store. It was there that my life changed forever.

I was always trying to come up with neat inventions to make the world more fun. One day I got the idea that plants could grow to be much more colorful if I mixed paint and fertilizer—so I did. The explosion could be heard for miles, and the entire city looked like the Partridge Family's bus—a beautiful sight. After the explosion something very strange happened. I became human, all except for my hair. I was amazed and shocked but I had no time to think, because a second can of paint was about to explode. All I could find quickly was a bag of twist ties and some duct tape. I used them to contain the paint, thus saving the city and the planet and . . . have I gone too far again?

Being human was strange, but somehow it felt right. I began wandering among the debris, collecting all kinds of cool things. With my trusty duct tape and twist ties by my side I began to fashion some of the debris into marvelous multi-colored inventions that everyone seemed to love. I had finally found my niche, so I hit the road and began performing in comedy clubs and colleges around the country .

Sometimes I miss being a carrot, but all that is left from those days is the top of my head. I had to come up with a new name for myself, so I became what you have all come to know me as—*CARROT TOP*.

That's it—the whole story. It's all true, I swear! Cross my heart, hope to die, stick a needle in my eye. . . . Are you convinced yet? Remember, imagination is the key to life and to this book, and as Einstein himself once told me (sure he did . . .) *imagination is more important than knowledge.*

PART ONE

HOUSEHOLD

Items

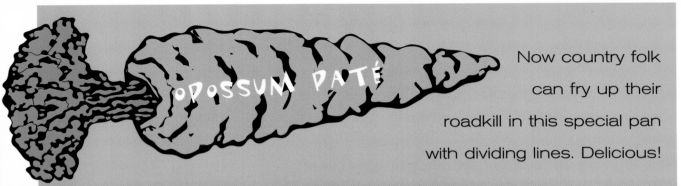

OPOSSUM PATÉ

Now country folk can fry up their roadkill in this special pan with dividing lines. Delicious!

My apron with a smoke detector on it will make even the worst cook a chef extraordinaire! I decided to invent it after my first home went up in flames.

Plate for
bulimics . . .
need I say
more?

6

FORK LIFT

Finally, overweight people can lose weight doing their favorite thing —eating. My new silverware with weights attached will turn you into a lean, mean, eating machine.

LEVEL-HEADED

Ice tray with a level on it so you won't spill the water before putting it into the freezer.

BOMBS AWAY

And so is Aunt Myrtle's potato salad when it hits the trap door that's built into this plate.

9

LOCK IN FRESHNESS

Tupperware with a calendar on it, for bachelors, so they know when their food grows penicillin.

"Let's see, I bought this in July of '93. Hey, it's still good."

10

If you come from a big family and don't want to drink out of the carton after everyone else, try my milk carton with the very hygienic quad-spout—everyone gets their own!

11

AN-Ti-Ci-PA-TioN

Don't waste time trying to put slow ketchup on fast food. My new ketchup bottle will slap it out for you.

SNOOZE, YOU LOSE . . .

. . . fingers, that is. My alarm clock with a guillotine will stop you from sleeping those extra minutes.

"Okay, okay, I'm up."

13

SLEEP LIKE A BABY

This pillow with built-in earmuffs will keep your dreams in and snoring out.

14

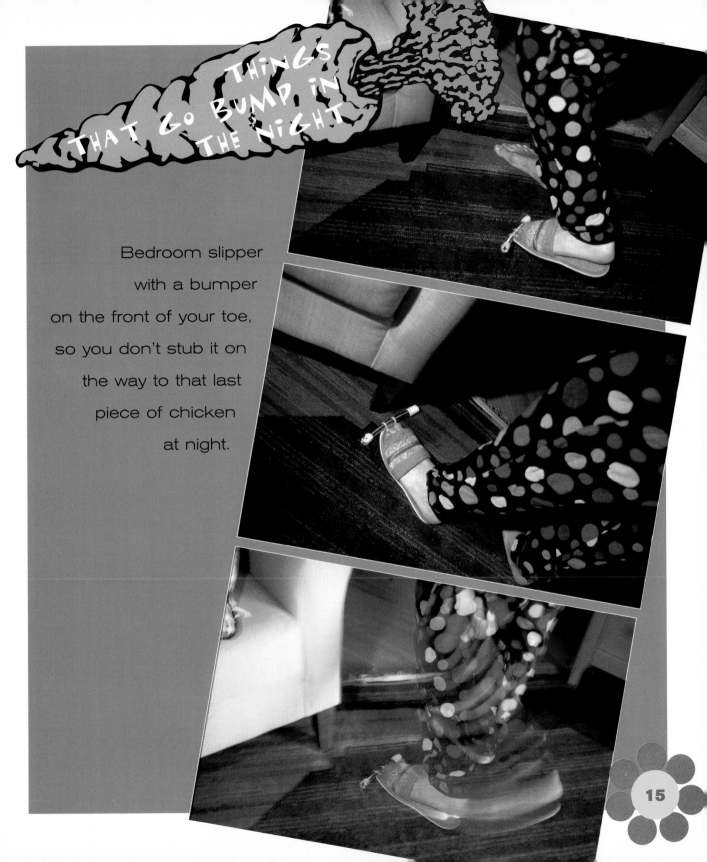

THINGS THAT GO BUMP IN THE NIGHT

Bedroom slipper
with a bumper
on the front of your toe,
so you don't stub it on
the way to that last
piece of chicken
at night.

15

No time to vacuum . . .

never fear . . .

Carrot Top is here!

It's a device that puts those vacuum marks on the rug.

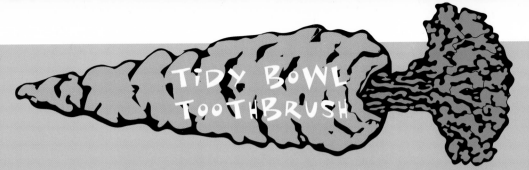

TiDY BOWL TOOTHBRUSH

Four out of five Democrats recommend it

. . . for Rush Limbaugh and other big mouths.

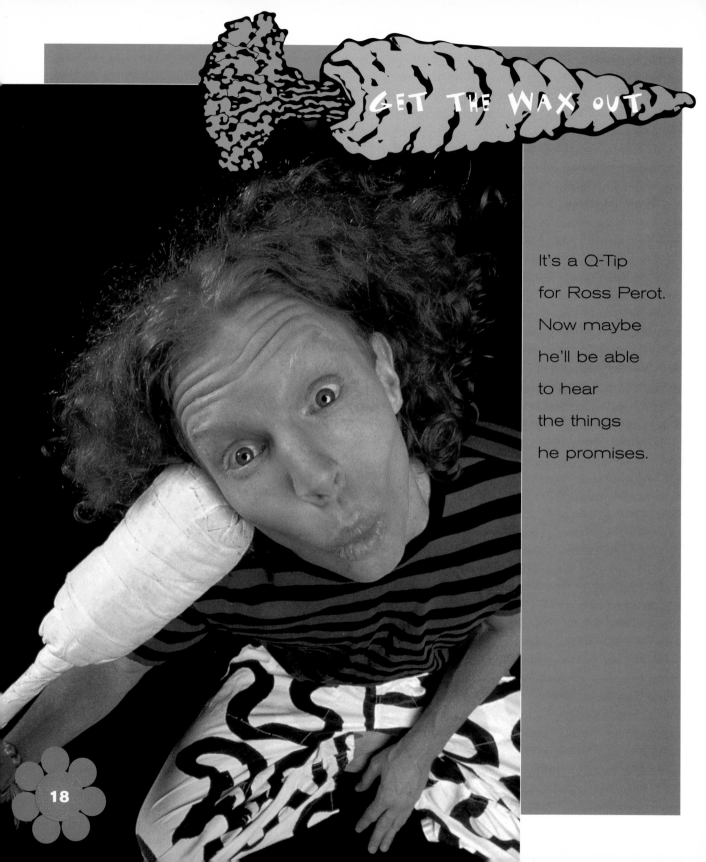

GET THE WAX OUT

It's a Q-Tip for Ross Perot. Now maybe he'll be able to hear the things he promises.

18

BUCKLE UP!

Toilet seat for a Mexican restaurant, so you can really strap yourself in for a ride.

"Okay, kids, it looks like it's going to be a rough one for Daddy."

19

A PROMISE TO GOD

Toilet seat so you can pray while you are throwing up.

"Please, Lord, help me live through this. I will never drink again. I really promise this time."

20

RAiN DROPS KEEP FALLiN'

Not anymore, ladies, thanks to this new toilet seat
that's wearing its own raincoat.

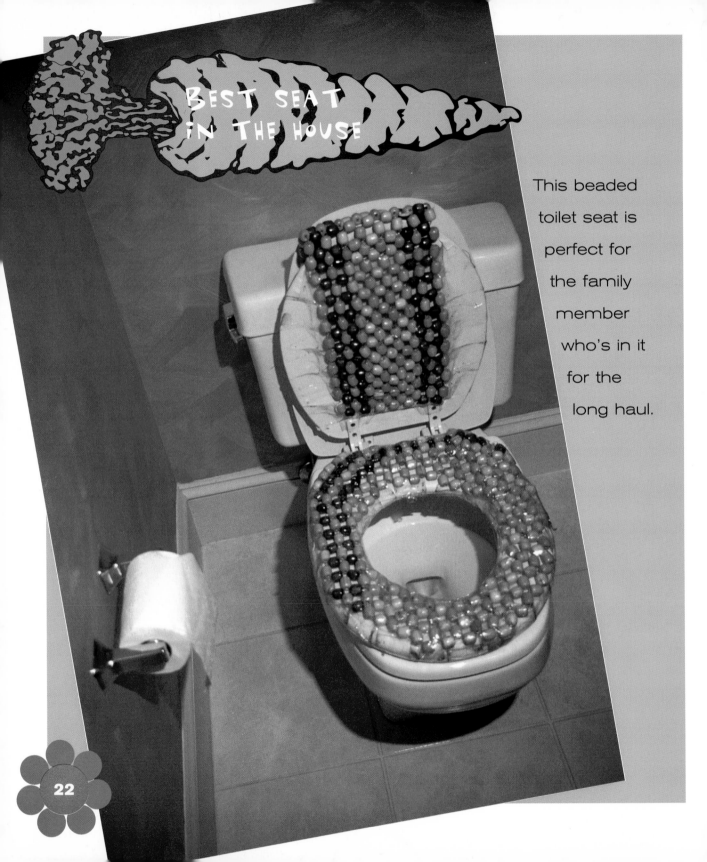

BEST SEAT
IN THE HOUSE

This beaded
toilet seat is
perfect for
the family
member
who's in it
for the
long haul.

Shower mat for men so they have something to aim for when they are peeing in the shower.

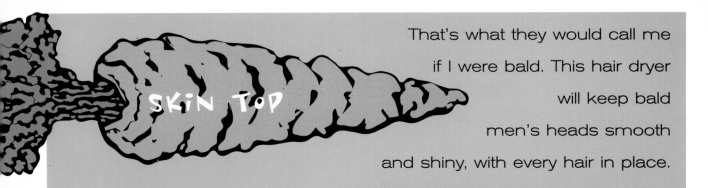

SKiN TOP

That's what they would call me
if I were bald. This hair dryer
will keep bald
men's heads smooth
and shiny, with every hair in place.

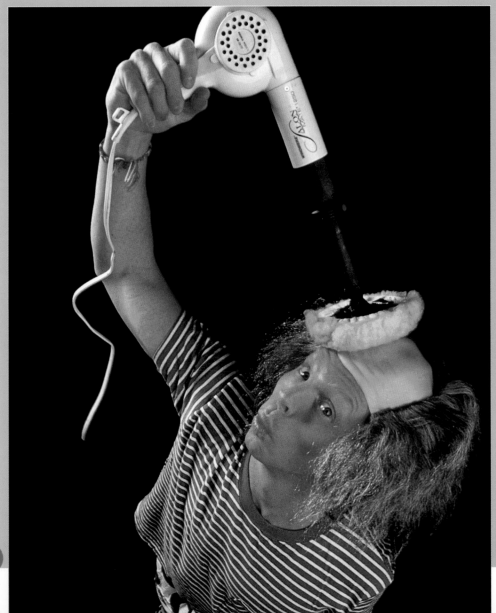

24

HiGH RoLLER

Combined toilet-paper dispenser/slot machine so you can gamble while going to the bathroom.

Ironing board in the shape of clothes so that it's easier to iron.

NO PLACE LIKE HOME

Mailbox for homeless people.

ENTER
AT YOUR OWN
RISK

A cheap
burglar
alarm! A
chalk out-
line of
some dead
dude in
your front
yard.

Another cheap
burglar alarm!
Just lay one
of these big bones
in your yard
and nobody
will ever break in.

BONE
HOME

DRAG STRIP

Now your dog will

have something to drag his butt across.

PART TWO

COPS and CARS

CLEAR A PATH

You'll never be late or lost again with this see-through map.

MIRROR, MIRROR ON THE . . .

At least you'll look good in the hospital if you use my rearview mirror with makeup lights. Designed for women drivers so you can put on your face even in rush-hour traffic.

MADE IN THE SHADE

Sun visor with sunglasses already attached so you won't lose them and you can look kind of cool, too!

IN THE RAT RACE

Here's something fun to do
—hang a bottle from your driver-side door
so you can drink like a gerbil at traffic lights.

ONE-ARMED BANDIT

Hey, look, it's a shirt I made so you don't sunburn your left arm during long trips in the car.

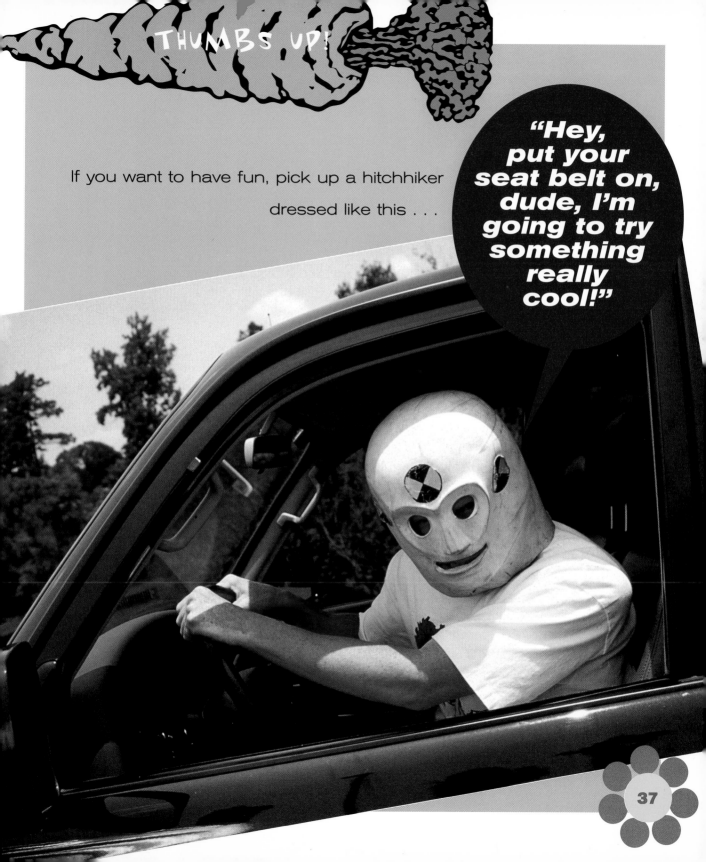

EASY RIDER

Helmet with hair on it so you can be cool
and safe at the same time.

38

I kept locking my keys in the car, so I just put them on a coat hanger.

DRiViNG
MiSS DAiSy

Hat for my
grandmother
to wear
when
she

is
driving
so her
head goes
above
the seat.

40

Rotating conveyor belt doughnut dispenser for cops, so when they pull you over you can offer them a fresh doughnut.

"Hey, that's a good choice there—that sprinkled one."

Krunchy Kram

41

CITIZEN'S ARREST

Hey, check it out! I made my own radar gun so you can tell the cop how fast *he* was going.

"I know, eighty-six. It must have gotten away from me."

Next time a cop pulls you over, just say,

"Hey, officer . . . speeding . . . really . . . me? . . . Oh, just put the ticket here with the other ones. I get them all the time."

43

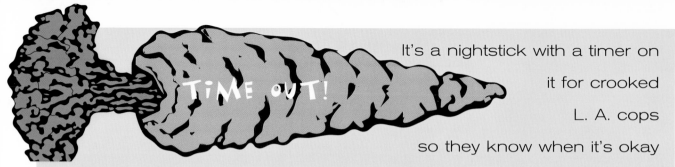

It's a nightstick with a timer on it for crooked L. A. cops so they know when it's okay to stop beating a citizen—I mean, criminal.

44

45

BREAKER, ONE-NINE

Hat with a siren for cops on bikes.

"Nothing worse than getting arrested by a cop on a bike and having to go to jail on the handlebars."

L.A.'S FINEST

Check it out. . . .

It's Mark Fuhrman's police belt!

STOP

Hat for hookers to help them get clients.

"I'll take the Hugh Grant special."

48

Here's something you can do for fun: drive around with this hanging out of your gas tank.

"Hey, you drove off with the gas handle!"

49

FULL SERVICE

Pull into the full service with this one hanging out of your gas tank.

"Fill 'er up, please."

50

PART
THREE

·

SpoRtiNg
GoodS

GET
A
GOOD
HIT

Tennis racket for Jennifer Capriati. Now I know why they wouldn't let her play at Wimbledon.

It has a grass surface.

MATCH POINT

That will be Monica Seles's new motto when she hits the courts. This new tennis racket with a rearview mirror will let Monica know what's happening on the other side of the net

. . . as well as

behind her baseline.

QUiET, PLEASE!

This tennis racket was designed especially for John McEnroe. Now his tantrums can be heard loud and clear.

54

ALL SKATE

Ice skates
for Nancy Kerrigan.

Ice skates for Tonya Harding.

55

GO DEEP

O. J. Simpson's football.

"Hey, go deep, honey. He cuts back, he slices and slashes his way to the end zone."

56

RUN, FORREST, RUN

Football cleats for rednecks.

"Air Bubba!"

IT'S UP ... IT'S GOOD!

Helmet for football kickers so they can tell which way
the wind is blowing before they kick the ball.

IN THE ROUGH

Next time your ball's in the rough and you give it a kick, use the Club Foot to get a better shot when no one's looking.

"Wow, nice shot, Ed."

59

AUSTRALIAN GOLF

What every golfer needs . . . a golf club with a boomerang on it so when you throw your club it will come back to you.

DOUBLE OR NOTHING

The Pete Rose
Commemorative
Baseball Cap

61

Baseball jersey with little rollers to help

ROLL UP TO THE PLATE

you slide.

62

CATCHING MONEY

Baseball glove with a calculator on it for Major League players, to give them something to do—calculate how many millions of dollars they are making while waiting in the outfield.

SIGN LANGUAGE

"Striiike."

Now catchers can communicate with pitchers without the batter catching on —with this multihanded chest protector.

FOUL BALL!

Don't take it hard in the jewels!
Wear my catcher's
pants . . .

"Aaah!"

. . . and keep
your valuables safe
and secure.

Moon River

66

WHO'S ON FIRST?

Don't let runners steal bases because you're too busy

looking for the signals. Now you can have eyes

in the back of your head!

67

Baseball bat for players so they can scratch their nuts and still concentrate on hitting the ball.

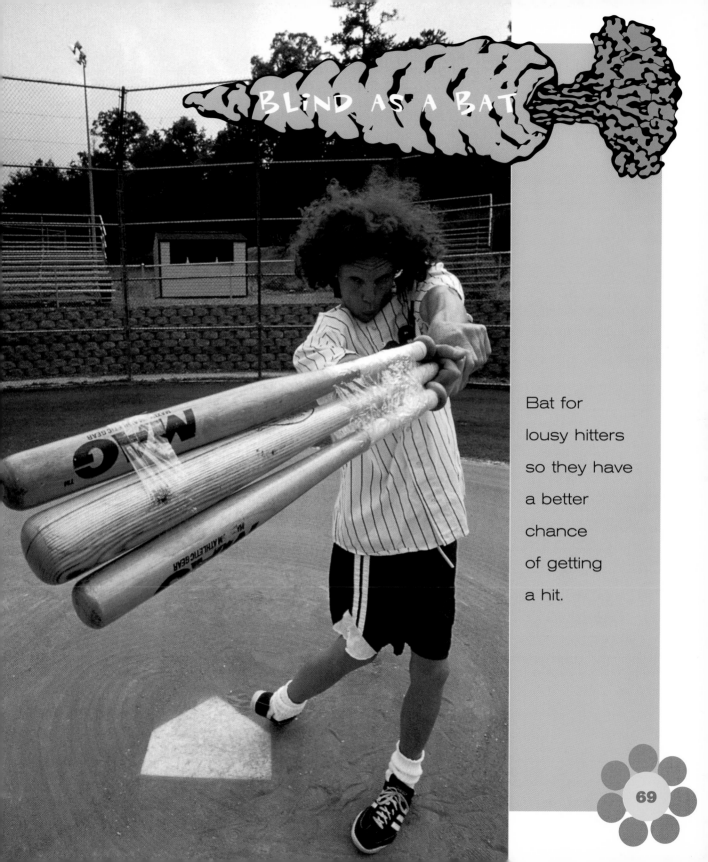

BLIND AS A BAT

Bat for
lousy hitters
so they have
a better
chance
of getting
a hit.

69

DEER CROSSING

Hat for hunters to wear so they can get closer to their quarry.

"Be vewy vewy quiet."

70

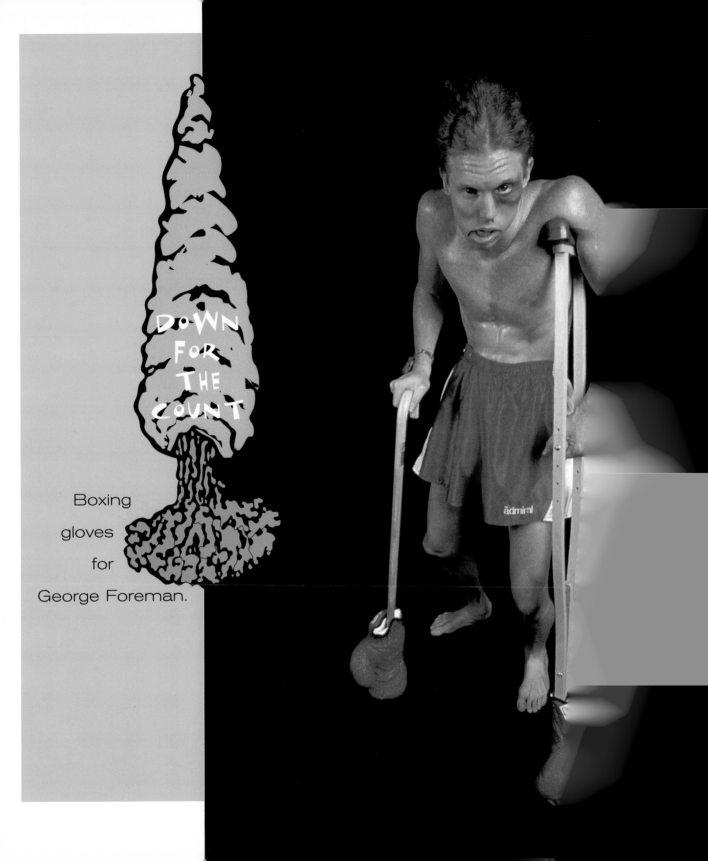

DoWN
FoR
THE
CoUNT

Boxing
gloves
for
George Foreman.

FUR BALL

Have fun at the park with my new Frisbee
—with a dog attached!

72

"Good catch, Corky."

WHEN NATURE CALLS

Hey, check it out—my camping belt.

My girlfriend's camping belt!

FREQUENT FLiER

Fly your bouquet
into the hands of anxious
bachelorettes with
this Frisbee Flower Flier.

PART FOUR

·

PARTY FAVORS

GOODBYE, DOLLY

You can haul
Bubba's drunk ass
out of the bar
with ease using
this new boot
with a built-in
hand truck.

I'VE FALLEN AND I CAN'T GET UP!

You won't get falling-down drunk again if you're wearing my new boot with a kickstand. Additional kickstands available for the serious partygoer.

PARTY ANIMAL

A party favor for people who have asthma.

Here's a great jacket to wear slam dancing, or just to get through crowded bars.

ON THE WAY TO THE MOSH PIT

NONSMOKER'S JACKET

Trying to quit smoking? Wear this jacket!

Every time you light up . . . beep, beep!

"Okay, okay, I quit."

DRINK UP, SENATOR

The fun never stops at the Kennedy compound.

Especially when Ted pulls out his personal shot glass.

UNHAPPY HOUR

Tequila bottle with an apology notepad attached. 'Cause you know you're gonna say some things you'll regret.

I'M SORRY

PART FIVE

FaShiON

DRESS FOR SUCCESS

You'll be ready for prom night in this stylish jacket covered with condoms.

EXPRESS MAIL

Jacket to wear to the post office in order to get quicker service.

"Excuse me, I think I'm next."

85

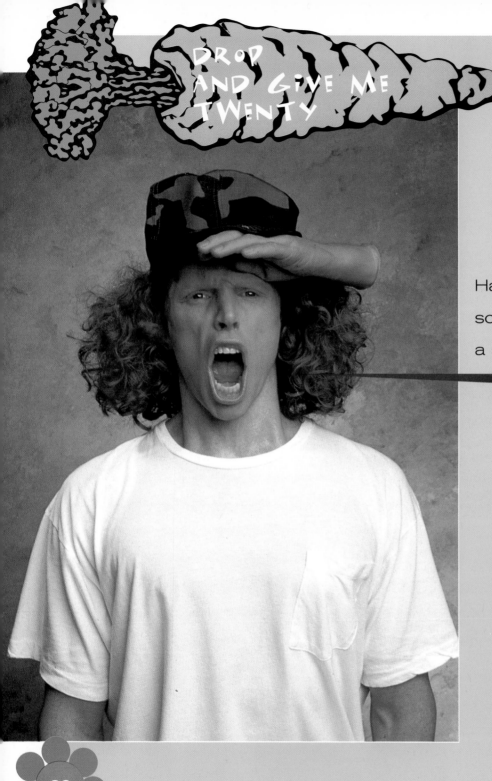

DROP AND GIVE ME TWENTY

Hat for the military so they won't miss a salute.

"Sir. Yes, sir."

CLEAN UP ON AISLE 7!

You won't have to worry the next time you're at the grocery store, because now Grandma's wearing the new turn-signal shopping belt!

87

I'M HOOKED

Thieves won't be able to grab and run when you're wearing this jacket. Walk the streets with confidence, ladies.

1. High heels for hippies.

2. High heels for truckers' girlfriends, so they can step into the cab easier.

3. High heels with training wheels, so beginners can practice.

4. High heels for rednecks.

THE LAW OF GRAVITY

Grandma's bra.

PART
SIX

·

ReDNeCkS

WATCH YOUR STEP

Hat for
rednecks
to wear
so they
don't spit
on the
sidewalk
when they
are dipping
chew.

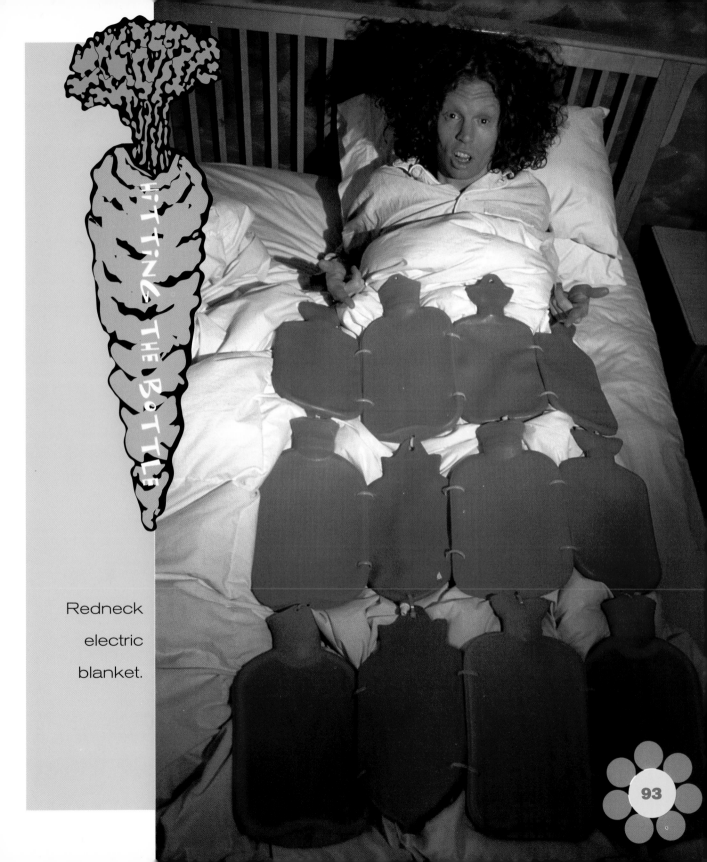

HITTING THE BOTTLE

Redneck electric blanket.

93

ERNEST & BUBBA GALLO

Redneck

wineglass.

VAL-E-HICK-TORIAN

Your parents will be proud when you beat the odds
and graduate from third grade.

95

PART SEVEN

SEVEN

MISCELLANEOUS

GENDER BENDER

Stencil for women to write their name in the snow.

MONA

Guitar for Willie Nelson so he can hide his money from the IRS.

I'M CHECKING MY BRIEFS

That's fancy lawyer talk. Check out my briefcase with a credit card machine built in—lawyers can haul it in. Made especially for Robert Shapiro and Johnny Cochran.

BE HEADED

Underwear for
John Bobbitt
to wear at night
so he can sleep
in peace.

101

Hey, this would be the perfect place for candidates to put their campaign promises.

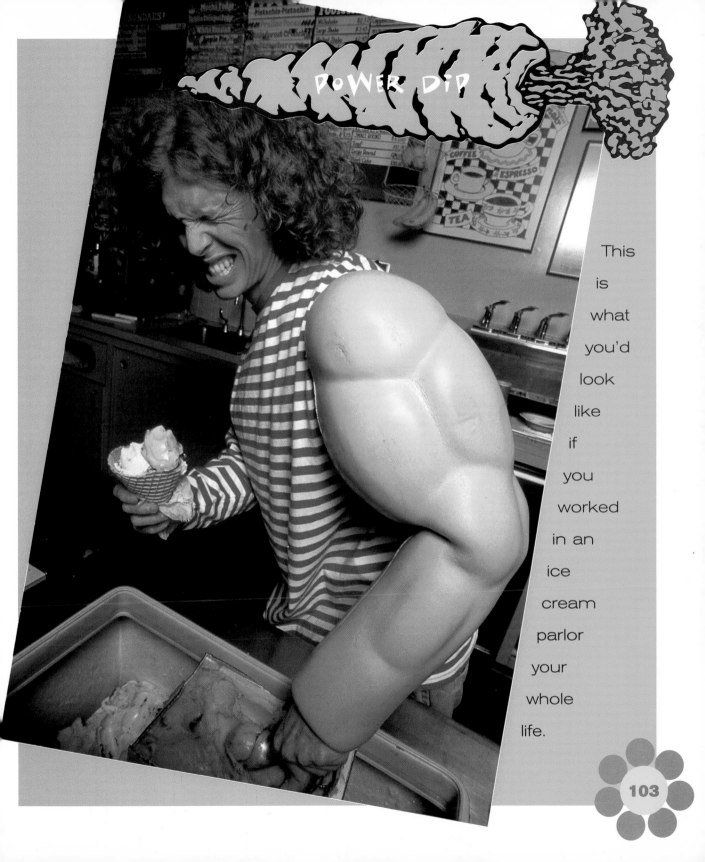

POWER DIP

This is what you'd look like if you worked in an ice cream parlor your whole life.

103

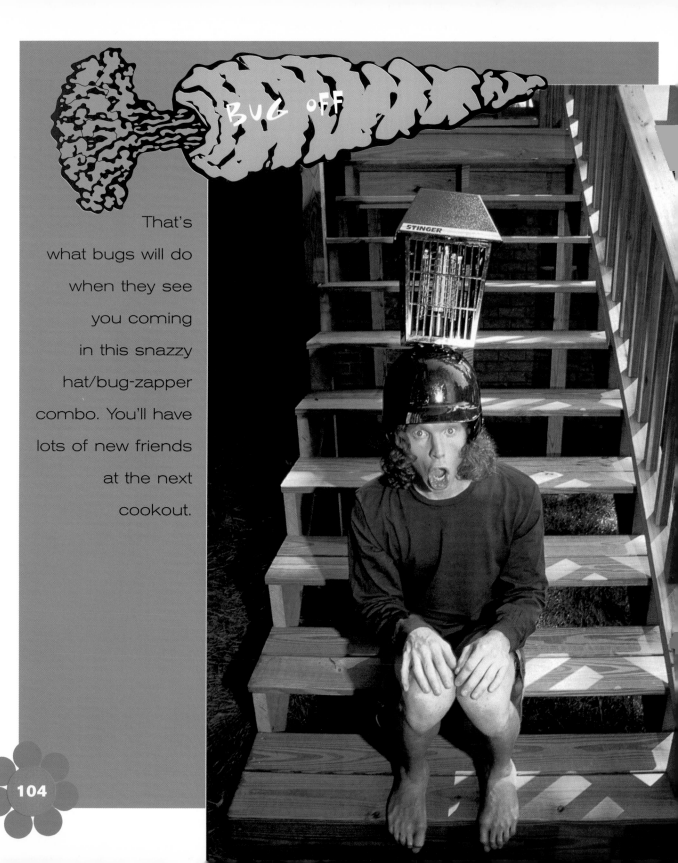

BUG OFF

That's what bugs will do when they see you coming in this snazzy hat/bug-zapper combo. You'll have lots of new friends at the next cookout.

STINGER

104

HOME...

It's a custom-made birdhouse for rich birds.

(I have way too much free time!)

HOME SWEET HOME

It's a custom-made birdhouse for redneck birds.

(I *definitely* have too much free time!)

107

WILL MOW FOR FOOD

Lawn mower for kids that has a meter on it so they can charge by the mile.

"Okay, Dad, 624 miles times $1.00. That's . . ."

$45.

108

Calculator for blondes.

Envelope for your

taxes.

PAY ATTENTION, CLASS.

The plight of underpaid teachers can now *change* with this new roll-book/collection-can combo.

SNACK PACK

With this new clear
lunchbox for inner-city kids,
the lunchroom will be
a much safer place . . . well,
except for the meatloaf.

JESUS SAVES . . . .

. . . and you will, too. This collection plate has a coin changer.

TWENTY-FOUR/SEVEN

KHASHISH-BAHLAWNY ABOU-CHAKRA

Name tag for convenience store employees.

GONE TO YOUR HEAD

This cozy heater attachment will stop your brain from freezing when you slurp down an icy drink too fast.

coldest drink in town

115

SCREAM, BUT NOT HEARD

I love children, and so will you with this new baby bubble hat. Perfect for airplane travel.

116

Presidential lie-detector podium.